THE STORE-HOUSE OF WONDER AND ASTONISHMENT

Praise for
SHERRY RIND
———

"In this collection of compelling persona poems, Sherry Rind gives voice to both the natural dignity and intelligence of animals, and to man's hubris which has shaped our relationships with them. Filled with deep compassion for other lives, these lyrical and often ironic poems show us how often humans 'narrowed in their single element' do not comprehend the varied ways of knowing in the non-human world. In this time in which widespread distrust of science has taken hold, her exploration of ancient writers' outlandish beliefs is a poetic mirror on our own ignorance. 'Because you cannot hear / you do not know how the earth talks to itself." *The Storehouse of Wonder and Astonishment* is a treasure trove of lyrical insight."

—ALICIA HOKANSON, author of *Perishable World,*
Mapping the Distance, and *Insistent in the Skin*

"An exquisitely written, compelling body of poems that anchors the world of animals to our transcendent human longing to know them, save them, be them. Or, at least, be as wildly innocent. 'We find the wild lands better than dreams.' Rind has skillfully created something original, a body of lyrical poems that read like rich, lavishly rich, gifts of delicate grace. The overall impression is that of a triumphant acknowledgment of animal life that takes the reader to a place of deep empathy and all-embracing tenderness.

—MARY LOU SANELLI, author of The *Immigrant's Table,*
Among Friends, and *Every Little Thing.* marylousanelli.com

ISBN 978-1-7364799-2-6
Library of Congress Control Number 2021946072

Cover and Book Design by Lauren Grosskopf

*Pleasure Boat Studio books are available
through your favorite bookstore and through the following:*
Baker & Taylor, Ingram, Amazon, bn.com &
PLEASURE BOAT STUDIO: A NONPROFIT LITERARY PRESS
WWW.PLEASUREBOATSTUDIO.COM
Seattle, Washington

The Store-House
of Wonder
and Astonishment

by Sherry Mossafer Rind

Pleasure Boat Studio:
A Nonprofit Literary Press

In memoriam

My mother, Bernice Mossafer Rind (1923-2018), who let me keep a dozen guinea pigs and much more.

My husband, John Welliver (1949-2000), who bought me my first budgerigar without knowing what he was starting.

And shining fish were given the waves for dwelling
And beasts the earth, and birds the moving air.
—Ovid's Metamorphoses

CONTENTS

III. Greatness in the Least Instruments

IV. That Science is Divine

INTRODUCTION

Beginning around the time of the first century CE, followers of the Judeo-Christian Bible generally viewed the natural world as a store-house of resources provided by a creator for the benefit of human beings. If Nature is a store-house, it is of wonders and, as we acknowledge 2,000 years later, of fragile and finite resources.

In these natural history poems, I have followed a tradition best described by John Ashton in 1890:

"Travellers see strange things," more especially when their writing about, or delineation of, them is not put under the microscope of modern scientific exam- ination. Our ancestors were content with what was given them, and being, as a rule, a stay-at-home race, they could not confute the stories they read in books. That age of faith must have had its comforts, for no man could deny the truth of what he was told. But now that modern travel has subdued the globe, and inquisitive strangers have poked their noses into every portion of the world, "the old order changeth, giv- ing place to new," and, gradually, the old stories are forgotten.

All the old Naturalists copied from one another, and thus compiled their writings. Pliny took from Aristotle, others quote Pliny, and so on; but it was re- served for the age of printing to render their writings available to the many...

Curious Creatures in Zoology.

I. TO TELL OF BODIES
Ovid

Elephants, Their Capacity

The elephant is the largest of them all, and in intelligence approaches the nearest to man. Pliny the Elder, 77 CE

We speak to the lines of sound
among planets, thin as spiders' silk,
when the new moon reveals itself
after the darkest night.

Silver to silver
we send up the water
and return to the forest.
Thus, we mark the years
of ascending and descending on earth.

When one of us falls,
we inhale her scent to keep it
with all the other stories;
the follower is not less than the leader.

When you take one of us
she will learn your language and obey
because she is no longer herself
but a dog whose world is work.
Because you fear our size
you diminish us.

Because you cannot hear
you do not know how the earth talks to itself.
You will never speak our language
which is of the earth
the deepest tides of underground streams
the molten shiftings you cannot hear.

Aristotle On the Disappearance of Birds

...these habits are modified so as to suit cold and heat and the variations of the seasons. Aristotle's *History of Animals*, 350 BCE

We account for the absence of certain birds in winter
through observation and travelers' reports. I have seen
cranes flying south in the fall,
their bodies the size of kites
in the great distance above us,
their horn-like call a musical reminder
of our diminishing season. As wealthy men spend
summer in cool places and winter in sunny ones,
cranes summer by the Black Sea and winter in Nile marshes
where they defend their eggs in battle
with goat-riding Pygmies whose spears
match in length the cranes' pointed beaks.
They drench the land in gore
with a ferocity Homer likened to a Trojan battle.

Our redstarts of summer disappear in winter
when robins are seen.
Note the similarity
in size and coloring:
the redstart's orange belly and undertail,
the slate head and back as if he dons a hooded cloak;
the robin's markings are muted
like winter's landscape.
We may assume the one transmutes into the other
to live more comfortably in each season.
From these birds
we learn the rhythms of time and weather.

Storks, kites, and doves fall into winter torpor
like their animal counterparts.
Swallows are nowhere to be found
and, like the redstarts, are too small to journey
from one land to another. Rather,
they sleep the winter through, hidden
in hollow trees or submerged in marsh-mud,
as men seek shelter in houses in winter.
Although fishermen may dredge hibernating swallows
from the depths, the birds soon die
if awakened before their time.

Left to natural desire in spring,
their beaks forge up through the silt
which flows off the birds
as they float to the surface
and leap joyfully
into the sky where they dip and dart
in the exuberance of spirits that all animals
display when once again sun warms the blood
and the season of growth stirs all creatures
to their natural cycles.
Only we who observe them
count the years to their inevitable end.

A Bed Among Goats

*You will have a warmer bed in amongst the goats than among the
sheep.* Aristotle

We press up during sleep, all dreaming
of new leaves. The kids' legs twitch in play.
Against the cold and the roaming panther
we need each other and the shepherd
sharing our warmth.

We bring cheer to horses,
who grow anxious about all they do not recognize;
a fallen branch is a snake,
a blown rag at the edge of vision,
the paw of a wolf. Among us,
their eyes stop rolling
and they bend their long necks to the grass.

We find the wild lands
better than dreams.
We climb high on a hill, high up broken boulders,
testing our clever feet.
Although buzzards hang above,
they are flies to us.

We do not fear these untried places.
Far below, olive trees wave silver and green,
whisper with the small birds
who never settle to their thoughts.

The shepherd comes after us, muttering,
watching her feet slipping among rocks
instead of looking out
where we look,
until we take pity and go to her.
We butt her legs gently, press up
until she lets go her human fears
and we return home as one.

Arkteia: acting the she-bear for Artemis

And clad in yellow robes, I was Little Bear to Brauronian Artemis.
Lysistrata, Aristophenes

We approach her shrine quickly
and marriage slowly
wearing robes the gold of bears tipped in sun.
On the vase paintings, we're all celebration
breasts and buttocks gibbous mooned
promising more.

Away from watchful families
we run through the woods.
Clothing flies off like flags
and the breasts men watched tremble
beneath gauze
retract as we bend close
to the ground
until all four feet
touch down
and claws tear up the dirt.

However sure-footed, we are unsure
in these new bodies, round and clumsy.
Where do we fit in the brambles,
hunched or upright, long limbed or short, both at once?

We split open a deer
and drink its blood
pouring the rest
for the goddess.
We never see the one we serve.

We imagine woman or monster
shaping in moonlight
where we bathe like the nymphs
we cannot be. We change again
to clothes, knowing
the transformations never stop
and we are always in service.

Dolphins

Among the sea-fishes many stories are told about the dolphin,
indicative of his gentle and kindly nature, and of manifestations of
passionate attachment to boys... Aristotle

They are warm. Seeing them
throw the sun in fragments
just where the surface licks
their many legs pushing
and bending like octopuses,
I come up from below to listen to their chirping;
their mouths bend in all directions
close to the waves. I sing to them
and slide my whole length along theirs.
When they slip down like falling fruit,
I nose them back up, watch
over them until they understand
their weaknesses, lives narrowed
in their single element.

Goat in the Wilderness

while the goat designated by lot for Azazel shall be left standing alive before the Lord, to make expiation with it and to send it off to the wilderness for Azazel. Leviticus 16:10 read on Yom Kippur

The stories grew for years—
that I met a demon
and fed him the human sins
tied to my horns with red wool,
that I was pushed off a cliff
screaming into the demon's maw,
that I wandered the desert
until, like the people, I forgot my slavery,

that I could not be the same goat
all these years later.
I am always the same goat.

They wonder what the demon looked like.
Do they know what a god looks like?
They want to think the demon has ram horns
and that it burns. Wouldn't I then be roasted meat
like the goat they sacrificed in their camp?

I ate the red wool they tied to my horns
and shat red pellets for days.
In the demon wilderness
I lost myself.

Everyone knows
nothing finds a way back
from the dead;

all bodies become food
for man, bird, or insect,
become white bones.
But the goat is never driven out.

Pliny Ponders News of the Phoenix

The birds of Aethyopia and India, are for the most part of diverse colours, and such as a man is hardly able to decipher and describe. But the Phœnix of Arabia passes all others. Pliny the Elder

I do not say this is true, only what I have heard.

There is never but one in the world
and no one reports seeing him.
The phoenix may number like other rarely seen birds
around whom tales grow like gossip.
Such may be the phoenix
whose story has traveled to Rome from Egypt and Arabia.

No one has reported
seeing the young of the sea-eagle in Rome in 500 years.
Amid the general heedlessness
to all knowledge which has of late prevailed,
it is more likely that no one has noticed them or the phoenix,
if it exists.

Manilius, famed for his immense learning,
gives the most detailed account of this bird:
the size of an eagle
with gold crest like a polished helmet
he raises into a plume;
below is a neck-plate of black-striped gold feathers.
The rest of the body, a deep red mixed with purple,
ends in an azure tail, all glowing when touched by sun.

Sacred to the sun-god in Arabia,
his life span is 540 years,
(coinciding with the revolution of our Great Year
when stars and planets return
to the positions whence they began).

When death comes,
he builds a nest with cinnamon and frankincense
and yields up his life.
From his decay climbs the tiniest worm,
which grows into a bird
whose first duty is to his father's rites, as it should be.
He takes up the whole nest
and carries it to the Temple of the Sun in Egypt,
placing it reverently upon the altar.

Cornelius Valerianus writes
that in the time of Claudius Caesar a phoenix was carried to
        Rome
to be shown to the public assembly.
Today nobody doubts this was a counterfeit phoenix,
though all the crowd believed the spectacle,
as crowds do.

What, then, is true?
Only that there is no end to the colors
found in birds, more various than an imperial garden;
their luster like polished metal
changes with degree and angle of light, as if
a creature transforms itself before our disbelieving eyes.

The Monster Hyena

*It is an easier matter to capture a male hyena, for in the females a
more crafty cunning is instilled by birth.* Gaius Julius Solinus,
3rd century CE

It is well known that the hyena imitates human sounds.
She summons dogs with counterfeit vomiting or whistling
and lures men from their huts by calling their names
at night in a woman's voice as sweet as any siren's
until they are far from help and lost in the bush
when the hyena leaps to devour them.

Her color yellowish, the blue spots bespeckling her sides
resemble eyes which make her
more terrible. Ignorant writers believed
the spots change color
but only the eyes themselves shift a thousand times a day
at the beast's pleasure.
The eye contains a stone rumored to give prophesy
if a man lay it under his tongue.

The credulous Aelian claimed the creatures change sex
from one year to the next, as a woman may change dress,
but Aristotle disproved such folly; however
a dog touching the shadow of a hyena will lose its voice.
Whosoever a hyena circles three times
will be struck stone-still and easily devoured.

So great is the vanity of the old magicians
that they declare the tooth of a hyena's upper jaw
will protect them from all darts and arrows.
If a man fasten the hyena's left foot to his arm,
he shall never forget whatsoever he hears or has ever known;

and if he wear the right foot,
whoever sees him shall fall in love with him.
The marrow of that foot when put in a woman's nostrils
will make her love her husband.
And in their folly, they believed
religious men send their souls into lions
and with their souls, women
animate the terrible hyena.

Pompey Takes Elephants to Rome for His Triumph Ceremony

Nay, there was even a certain feeling of compassion aroused by it,
and a kind of belief created that the animal has something in common
with mankind. Cicero, 55 BCE

In Rome we pleased them with games,
our trunks stronger than bows
hurling arrows straight and true against the wind.
We walked a tight-rope to show how they misjudged
our grace and stepped neatly among them
when they toppled in their wine like fruit
rotting in the dirt, until they rose

to their malevolence. Walls of men
surrounded us in the arena; their thousand, thousand shouts
crazed us against the men throwing rocks and spears.
We had no choice
but to stomp them back into earth,
painting ourselves with their blood.

Then came hunters whose acid smell we knew
from home. One speared our leader's eye.
We had no time to see the life go out of him.
They pinned our feet, hacked
our trunks and throats, cut the tendons in our legs.
Our tears and blood ran ditches in the ground.
We rammed the walls
which shook but did not fall.

The last of us raised our heads
and reached our trunks to the gods.
We sang out lamentations
until the people sang with us and the spears stopped.
We touched our kin good-bye. Their bones
scattered across a continent not ours
and the shame breathed through us until we died.

Scitalis

The snake called scitalis gets its name because it glitters with such a variety of colour. Aberdeen Bestiary, 1200 CE

She cannot join your drinking parties,
your warm rooms lit by fire.

Beneath notice
she puts all effort into her dress,
gold and diamonds,
a glimpse of peacock blue leaving you

hunting for the rest of the bird
or maybe a butterfly,
you think.

Blinded by sunset pink and copper
you slow.
She's just here, down here
among the multitudes

the mud and moss where desire starts.
It tricks you awake, holds you

mesmerized. And then
she has you.

Undermined

The inhabitants of the Gymnesian islands sent a deputation to the Romans soliciting that a new land might be given them, as they were quite driven out of their country by these animals. Strabo, Geography, 1st century CE

Between the seed and the harvest
the rabbits
sculpted lettuce and beet greens
into signs
atop the inverse roadmap
of their tunnels.

If we stumbled at our doorsteps
we said the rabbit below
shifted in his sleep.
Between our reach and grasp
hopped the rabbit.

In the watery space before sleep
we saw brown, wondering eyes
and pink-lined ears.
Trees leaned, then toppled
and floors sagged.
Between the fear and the action
came the rabbits.

We ate rabbit
we sent rabbit
to the hungry multitudes of Rome
we brought ferrets from Africa
to hunt rabbit
but still the squirming carpet of them
pushed into our homes.

We petitioned the emperor
to send the army
or give us a new island.
The birds flew off
for lack of trees
and we loaded our ships
checking between cookware and clothes
for the rabbits.

We cut our community to fragments
wriggling into whatever
towns would have us.
Our language died
as did the rabbits at last.

Between the bones of our buildings
and the bones of rabbits
came rosemary, fennel, and brome.

Castor

He throws away that, which by natural instinct he knows to be the object sought for... Gerald of Wales, *The Itinerary of Archibishop Baldwin through Wales,* 12th Century CE

The one who draws the short straw
must lie on his back and accept
all the timber piled on his belly,
arms and legs held up like the sides of a cart
and his mouth stuffed with sticks
before his compatriots drag him by the tail
to their river den where several families
together make their dwellings
wherein they sleep upstairs when the water rises
and below when water recedes.

Like the frog or seal, these animals
remain under water at their pleasure,
guided by broad, thick tails.
Because this part is naked, great
and religious persons in time of fasting,
eat the tails as having both the taste and color of fish.

The beaver digs dry hiding places in the river bank
and when he hears the hunter
seeking him with sharp poles thrust down the dirt,
he flies to the defense of the castle;
but if he cannot elude the hunter and his dogs,
he will ransom himself. In the hunter's sight
he castrates himself with his teeth
and throws the testicles to the man
who will sell them for medicine.
If the hunter pursues a castrated beaver,
the animal at an elevated spot lifts his leg
to show the object of desire is gone.

The beaver has but four teeth, two above and two below,
broad and sharp to cut like an axe.
When a beaver can get hold of a man,
he will not let go
until he hears the fractured bones
grating beneath his teeth.

Relative to the Mole

And, it is said, they can even understand it if you talk about them.
Pliny the Elder

Neighbors,
when pursuing his ordinary work of swimming through dirt
to aerate lawns and loosen soil, the mole
can make any of us an eyesore,
the value of our ownership weakened,
our perfect care scorned.

Although you may never welcome him,
consider his history.
When your lawn rises in hills and ridges,
one animal is weaving a maze
once thought a ward against evil.
His kind has suffered at our hands,

not only the bleach and water
hosed down his tunnels, the gas, mothballs, and poison
but also the sacrifice of the body.
Caught at night when he rose to take the air,
a tooth pulled from a living mole and worn as a necklace
stopped toothache. A sprinkle of his blood cured delirium.

Swallowing his still-pulsing heart
(very small, it slips down)
imparted the gift of divination.
The rest would not go to waste. Dried,
his long-nailed hands kept always in a pocket
guarded against rheumatism and epilepsy.

Those who would be healers
squeezed out his life with their hands,
the soft fur, the human-feeling paws going limp
against theirs. Neighbors, can you say none
of your ancestors partook?
Can you say you believe nothing?

II. WONDERS WHICH NATURE HATH GIVEN
Gonzalo Fernández de Oviedo

The Kinde of Hyaena Called Papio

And there was one of these in Germany in the year of our Lord 1551 at the City of Auspurg [Arnsberg].... It was of a cheerful nature, but then especially when it saw a woman, whereby it was gathered that it was a lustful beast. Edward Topsell, *The History of Four-Footed Beasts,* 1607

My Dear Margarete,

I made a most unusual friend, although I don't know if you would call friend one who steals my lunch or handkerchief as easily as breathing. He lived in the park trees and took joy in shaking fruit down on our heads.

The traveler who brought him said others of his tribe have long tails, carried upright like flags. Ours arrived with a short tail, the result of some injury, possibly during capture. He grew to the size of a large dog, with a dog's snout, yet he would spend long periods of time sitting up like a person. His hands startled me, four fingers long and slender, nimble as any seamstress', but with a small thumb.

He was more likely to approach a woman than a man. I believe he preferred women's softer voices, as do some dogs. Nor would women stand over him and try to stare him down or stalk toward him, all hulking shoulders, until he bared his sharp, canine teeth and fled up a branch. We would approach him like the child he was and take satisfaction in seeing him cheerful. He delighted in apples, plums, and other fruits. The music of a pipe or timbrel was a sure way to draw him close; he listened with more dedication than any audience you have seen in a musical evening.

One day he jumped to the arm-rest of the bench where I sat in the park. I held out the pear I was eating, for I would rather give than have it taken. We looked into each other's faces, his eyes round and amber-brown with small black pupils. The world stilled. You know I keep many animals, but never have I felt I was looking into their faces as one equal to another, on the very edge of words.

Then he took the pear as neatly as any gentleman and sat back to eat it, the two of us gazing across the park like friends of such long duration that we need not speak. Finished, he sprang up into the tree.

And that is all! You may think me silly to set such store by one look and that not exchanged with a lover. I have broken off with Karl, by the way. He laughed at my calling a monkey "friend."

That friend died last month from afflicted lungs.

So I will leave this place. That is what his eyes told me, of a world beyond my own, of dust and grasses, of far-reaching trees black against an orange sky, of vista itself instead of this closed-in place where the only wildness is a cultivated park of trees and flowers in regular rows. I will send you details of my escape. I wish you may experience, even once in your life, this desire, this certainty.

Much Love,
Hette

Common Potoo

Do not prevent us from hearing the good news that our grandfathers are even now announcing to us; for when we hear these birds, we all rejoice and receive renewed strength. Tupinamba elder to Jean de Léry, *History of a Voyage to the Land of Brazil*, 1578

In the bird's four falling notes
we hear the dead whose souls dance
behind the far mountains, and in the vigil
between songs our minds range the forest
with the jaguar, the insects of earth and air,
the snakes who never close their eyes in sleep.

The bird tells us to listen
for the hush of bodies through moss and fern
and on branches where they slip between leaves
so smoothly that they do not stir the air.
We hear life beginning and ending.

The dead are hidden like this bird
who blends with bark on broken trees by day
and cries far through the forest at night.
The dead have lost their voices
but in the bird's chant we hear
the stories of their names.

A Brief Account of Venomous Creatures

It does appear very wonderful that, when anything venomous is
brought there from other lands, it never could exist in Ireland.
Giraldus Cambrensis, *Topography of Ireland,* 1188

Though it be a flattering fiction that the saints
cleared these islands of all pestiferous animals,
it is more likely they never existed here any more than wolves.

We suspect green germs of life float in the air,
wet as it is, cleansing all who dwell here,
for the people never sicken until death.

The Venerable Bede, not to be doubted,
tells us every reptile and serpent carried from Britain
dies immediately it breathes the wind

blown from Irish shores
and every poison introduced from other countries
loses its malignant effect, as if turned to rain.

Bede himself witnessed people serpent-bit in England
given scrapings from the leaves of Irish books stirred in water
whereupon the venom lost its power and the swelling drained.

So hostile is Ireland to poison
that its dust sprinkled on foreign gardens
will drive away every venomous reptile.

Indeed, if all Britain knew these miraculous properties,
then neither book nor speck of soil
would be left in Ireland.

Of a Frog Lately Found in Ireland

There are neither snakes nor adders, toads nor frogs, tortoises nor
scorpions, nor dragons. Gerald of Wales, *Topography of Ireland,*
1187

No man supposes this reptile was born in Ireland
for its mud does not contain the germs
from which green frogs are bred,
though some particle may have been exhaled
with moist soil into the hollow of a cloud
by the quickening heat of our atmosphere
and blown to Irish shores—
for most clouds go to Ireland—
and dropped in the ungenial soil
where the frog succeeded long enough
to astonish both the English governor and the Irish
when it was found near Waterford
and brought to court still alive
whereby the King of Ossory beat his head in grief
and said this frog portended the invasion of the English
for the subjugation of his people.
Even as he spoke, the frog expired.

Isidore of Seville Comments on Crows

It is a great sin to believe that God would entrust his counsels to crows. Isidore, Archbishop of Seville, *Etymologies*, 7th century CE

When the world does not function to its liking
the crow's voice grinds
all day until it tires.

If you throw a stone at a crow
he will remember and scold your disregard
when he sees you leave your house.

So should you scold the devil
who tempts you from truth
and circles you with confusion.

Augurs endow the bird with human cares,
say crows warn us where ambush waits
and tell the future in discordant song.

All birds, when they fly, pursue a straight path
unencumbered by hill, tree or fence.
They see much that is hidden from us,

but it does not follow that they tell
what they see on roads or in the future.
A sailor predicts rain as well as any crow.

Some say a crow brings gifts,
others that a crow on the roof predicts ill fortune,
but the faithful know our sins cause calamity.

Crows clear our walkways of dead vermin
not for our benefit
but for themselves and their young.

Parents escort their fledglings into the difficult world
and see them safe to perches long after self-sufficiency.
Here is prediction: all young will thrive with unremitting care.

When a flock member dies, crows circle the corpse
as we keep watch over our dead.
Obsequies finished, they disappear into the clouds

as if they have some converse with heaven. But
do not think God speaks with crows above your clergy.
Do not put faith in birds.

Archdeacon Cambrensis' Lessons from the Birds of Ireland

Can any good come from Ireland? Gerald of Wales

1. Of Barnacles, which grow from fir timber

There are likewise here many birds called barnacles, which nature produces in a wonderful manner…

Of the myriad forms of propagation
that of the Barnacle Goose is most remarkable.
They lay no eggs nor raise goslings
but generate like fruit on a tree.
At first they appear as lumps of pine pitch
before enlarging their white shells
striated with black, suggestive in color, size and shape
of the geese's heads and the striping on their backs and wings.

Clinging with the long stalk of beak and neck
and floating with a current-tossed log like sea weed
the fetal birds and tiny feathers grow safely
nourished most miraculously by the wood's juices
until large enough to free themselves and swim on the waters
or launch into the air for the journey to landfall.

As the shell represents the form and markings of the goose,
so Nature demonstrates symmetry in creation
wherein the Maker repeats patterns like an artist
for our appreciation and humble edification.
With the Barnacle Goose engendered of wood
and the bee bred from the honeycomb,
Nature affirms, like the pastor in his sermon,
the original power of the holy spirit.

But the Jew, whose arrogance is as constant as the sun,
who dares not deny the first man begotten from clay
and the woman from man alone, as written
in his Old Testament, with obstinate malice denies
His holy procreation from female without male;
and sows the seeds of his own destruction
in the face of Nature's irrefutable argument for our faith.

2. Of the crane and its nature

The liver of this bird is also of such a fiery heat that, when by any
chance it swallows iron, its stomach digests it.

In their flocks of hundreds, cranes
keep watch in turns at night for their common safety.
They perch on one foot and hold up a stone in the other
that if they should fall asleep, the fall of the stone
from their relaxing foot will rouse them to renew the watch.

These birds are emblem of the bishops of the church,
whose office it is to keep watch over their flock.
At any hour the snake may insinuate itself
into the congregation and tempt the innocent
to evil deeds—immoral unions, thievery, calumny—
for it is the nature of man to sin.

Sacred duty is like the stone clasped to the bosom
ready to drop and alert the mind to danger.
Then the crane points its daggered bill toward heaven
with resounding cries that alarm the hearts
of the flock and impel them to safety.

Thus does the pastor with unwearied diligence
drive evil from the fold
by sounding the alarm from the holy oracle
and summoning his people to hear. Even thunder
crashing on the roof of the church
cannot command more attention.

Lightning cleaves the tree
and the fiery heat of the crane's liver melts iron
but no more than bowels inflamed with the fire of faith
subdue hearts which were obdurate
and move them to soft concord in brotherly love. Then
like the brown lark which rises from the dirt
where it dwells unremarked, all sing
Heaven's praise in pure voice.

3. The nature of the osprey

There are also many birds here of a twofold nature....

Who can trust the osprey's intent?
One foot is harmless, fit only for swimming,
and the other spreads open with talons
armed for taking prey.

I have witnessed these birds hovering
in the air over the waves, still and certain
as the north star which guides us at night.

Their vision cleaves the great space of turbulent air and water
to small fishes lurking in the sand beneath the waves.
With headlong speed, the osprey dives
fearlessly into the depths
It uses its webbed foot for swimming
while the talons of the other pierce and seize its prey
carrying it off to unknown heights.

In like manner, mankind's old enemy
fixes his keen eyes on us
however we may try to conceal ourselves
in the trouble-tossed waves of this present world
and ingratiates himself with soft tread
before clutching miserable souls with his taloned other foot
and dragging them to perdition
where there is no deliverance from the consequences of sin.

4. Of martinets and their natures

For degenerating here, they have the belly white with a dark-coloured
back....

The kingfisher, here called martinet, dives in the water
after the small fish on which it feeds.
Like parrots and peacocks, the back and wings distinguish
a lustrous shade of green
which in some lights is blue,
as the faith of good men may appear in one guise or another.

If preserved in a dry place when dead, they never decay
any more than the words in the great book
that never lose their luster.
Laid among clothes, their bodies warn off the moth
and impart a pleasant odor. More wonderfully,
if the dead birds are hung by their beaks in a dry situation
they renew their plumage yearly,
as if restored to life.

Thus holy men, who are dead to the world
and, as it were, laid up in a dry place,
purify themselves and those who are united with them
from being corrupted by sin
and render them conspicuous by the odor of their goodness.

While they hang from above,
casting off the old garment of flesh
and clothed in new virtues,
they are changed and renewed for the better.
For that is the highest pitch of excellence
when life is cast off and the soul rises to its greatest union
with the yearning of birds for the sky.

Lupus Est In Fabula*

The wolf has no friends but the parrots. Edward Topsell

In youth he kills the stag
and then the sheep men claim as theirs.
Toothless in old age
he scratches for meat in the trash heaps and houses
of the city. Even if tamed
he hates the master who looks upon him.

If a wolf is first to see a man
the man will lose his voice.
To stop the attack
he must strip off his clothes
and bang two rocks together.
When a man struck a wolf with his club
she leapt and clawed the skin off his face.
Once healed, the man began to howl like a dog.

A wolf's heart burned and beaten
to powder and taken in drink
will stop the thrashings of falling-sickness.
His canine tooth rubbed on the gums
of infants will open them up
for the teeth to grow through
without pain.
The wolf ate the pain.

The wolf has no friends but the parrots
who gaze down like gods.
They drop fruit in his path
to ease his toothless old age.
When he dies
they send his voice through the trees and
everyone falls silent at once.

Saint Ambrose Admonishes

Whereas [crows] offer even their own lives for strangers, we close our doors to them.... Whereas the storks consider these as their defenders, we frequently treat them as enemies. Ambrose of Milan, *Hexameron,* approx. 387 CE

When the year begins to close,
storks in migration do not rise
like wind-tossed leaves

but, following the guidance of crows,
advance in precise ranks
of military pageant, their wings its banners,

their guardians ready to battle any birds that close
against them and to see their charges safe to winter roosts.
The crows do not linger in pleasant climes

but, covered with the wounds
of bitter conflict, return to the cold, crying out
encouragement and pain to one another.

Is there punishment for desertion from this dangerous bond?
To keep from harm, do some crows hide as the rest fly off?
No, each strives to outdo the others in his allotted task.

Whereas crows offer their own
lives for those not of their flock, we bar our doors
and hide as if in fear. We shirk the duty owed

the stranger and the oppressed (except
the Jews whom we consign to the flames
for their refusal to be saved in the sight of Our Lord).

Although animals lack the wit to question their lot,
we with superior powers are raised above all others
to reject their ways or honor them as beacons

rising in a world granted as our dominion.
Following, we claim the wealth
found even in the wings of birds.

Apes

As he is very like to man in several parts of his body, so he doth strive to imitate mens actions, but very foolishly. Wolfgang Franz, *The History of Brutes*, pub. 1670

The chimpanzee traced the yellow thread
through a cat's-ball tangle of multi-colored string
to the peanut tied at the end
and scored points
on the intelligence scale along with
her peanut. The gorilla
turned her head away
to gaze out the window
at poplars flipping their leaves gray and green
in the wind. The benevolent souls
giving tests thought gorillas less
intelligent, later learned
gorillas do not care for puzzles
or the flashing squares that yield
one miserly peanut, keeping
chimpanzees occupied and out of trouble
like the people at bingo machines
but needing more concentration.
Gorillas deliberate
like chess players,
like Leah who studied the muddy pond
before finding a stick to sound the depth
for each step she took
and Effi who judged the force of water
and laid a plank bridge to cross a ditch.
Among gorillas, the women
lever the world, use sticks
to pry apart wires, reach food.
They do not care for applause;

clapping hands
means *come play.*

The Reverend Alexander Ross Explains Griffins

*Besides, though some fabulous narrations may be added to the story
of the Griffins, as of the one-ey'd Arimaspi with whom they fight, yet
it follows not that therefore there are no Griffins.* Alexander Ross,
*Arcana Microcosmi,*1652

At the edge of the inhabited world
where all things most rare and beautiful are found,
near the cave of the north wind, Boreas,
that violent old man of wings and ice-spiked hair
whose sighs hurl men off mountains,
where griffins build their lairs high above his cave,
the Arimaspi men whose desire has no end
crawl up in search of gold.

A thousand men wait for a moonless night
to invade with spades and sacks
but if one should ring the silence with iron on stone
the sharp-eared griffins rise on thundering wings.
Plucked up like mice, men break
with cries that rumble down the mountainsides.

Made wealthier by danger, those who escape with gold
say the griffin is lion bodied with an eagle's head,
claws the size of drinking cups,
black feathers along its back,
white wings, and eyes like fire. Do they fly
or leap with claws outstretched
so far that those who fall in terror
believe them airborne? Do their eyes burn red
or reflect mere firelight?

Though fearsome beasts grow larger in the mind,
it does not follow that they cannot be.

If any say such animals as griffins
are not found in our civilized world,
I say that may be true
for they live in places so remote—
and many there still are—
that Europeans dare not pursue
and only stolen gold descends into our hands.

Horse Latitudes

These animals possess an intelligence which exceeds all description.
Pliny the Elder

As conversationalists, she said, the horses
grow monotonous, telling
the same stories as the day before
or last week, like the one
about the horse walking into a bar
and she chuckles at the punch line
every time to keep them jolly
after the time she interrupted with
"What do you call ducks in a box?"
and they walked away from the fence where she leaned,
their rumps toward her, brown and white. Those two
she said, have each other, together
long enough to hold whole conversations
in an eyelid twitch, a head nod, which
every time she sees, she feels that stomach-dropping
anxiety of emptiness, the perpetual
half-life of an uncoupled animal
like a duck she knew years ago
who, when the drake died, quacked
all day and night
a sound that used to be silly but now
a heartbreak cry spread across the acres
until she, the human, brought in a new drake
whereupon the duck's cries turned to murmurs.
The horses don't understand, she said,
what it's like to be unknown and unnamed
without anyone who'll chat
even if you don't bring carrots.
But she continues
to fork hay and shovel manure because

there's no one else
to do it.

The Tiger of Glorious Form

So great is the swiftness of this beast...that some have dreamed it was conceived by the winde. Edward Topsell

Three appeared in the park at dusk
slipping along wooded trails like the lengthening shade.

Given weapons they carried like baskets
the crew saw a tiger break from the laurels

and race up the path. Hearts hammered
and the juices of their fear electrified.

The people must be locked up.
Outside the park, teenagers still play in the lake.

An old lady saw a tiger pass through her kitchen;
no one believed her. She will stay in the pub

until all are gone. They could be anywhere
in the large park. Small dogs have disappeared.

If they taste us
they will want us forever.

Tomorrow we must tie a goat in the clearing
and not mistake light fingering the leaves
for a tiger.

The Lives of Northern Bears

Dancing Lithuanian Bears

Russians and Lithuanians…consider it a rare pleasure to have near them the wildest animals, so well tamed that they are utterly obedient to their owner's every whim. Olaus Magnus, *A Description of the Northern Peoples,* 1555

When captured bears are chained
or caged until hunger makes them amenable,
men may stroke and play with them
while holding the promise of food.
Sweet pipe music induces the bears to follow
their trainers in comical dancing and gestures.

The bears learn to walk on their hind legs
and hold out begging cups in their fearsome claws
to their audience of married ladies and young girls.
If an audience prove ungenerous, a sign from the trainer
sets the bears growling and shaking their heads
until income is satisfied.

Noblemen sent their sons with wandering shows
to learn far-off countries' customs and defenses
until reports of wayfarers robbed and thrown
to starving bears ended the custom.

After the show season, bears earn their keep
by turning well-wheels for the households of lords.
Their great strength raises
such large buckets that two fill a tub.
Bears haul ploughs and carry sacks and logs
more faithfully than any servant. Those of much gravitas
guard the gates of important men
from wolves and other dangerous animals.

Bears at Sea

Captive bears are brought on board ship and display a series of entertaining gymnastics as they climb up and down the cables.

When an approaching pirate saw strong men scaling
the rigging as if preparing for defense,
he turned his ship away from attack and never knew
he had seen but young bears sporting.

When bears look out to sea like any sailor
propping his arms on the rails, whether pleased
at the choppy waves or searching for an end to the void,
seals entranced by the sight encircle the ship
and the sailors fall upon them with harpoons.
Those remaining in the water are caught as well
when they leap to the aid of comrades squealing like pigs.

Ways to kill thieving bears

As it is so voracious, local people time and again put it to death...

1.
Here bees thrive in such abundance
that domestic hives cannot house them all
and their owners encourage them to swarm
to forest trees hollowed by nature or human skill
where insatiable bears climb to steal honey.
With skulls as fragile as a parrot's beak,
they are easily killed.

The farmer will suspend a cudgel studded with iron spikes
above the hole from which bees emerge.
The bear will dislodge it in his impatient search

and down it will fall on the lawless creature.
In exchange for the loss of some small amount
of honey, the farmer earns the hide, the meat,
and the bear's fat which heals wounds.

2.
In autumn, when fruit ripens in red clusters on trees
the bear must stand erect to pull the branches down
and so intent is he on stripping the fruit that he never hears
the hunter's crossbow snap.
Struck with arrow and alarm,
the bear ejects like hailstones behind him
all the berries he has eaten before he turns to run.

But the hunter has placed there a dummy man
which the bear tears apart with long claws. Now
the hunter fires the fatal arrows, and even as he dies
the bear roars and paws the air in terrible fury.

3.
A bear will leap onto a bull's back
and grip its horns and shoulder blades with all her claws
until it sinks, on the verge of death.
Then she hoists it on her back like luggage
and carries it toward the forest, never thinking
she leaves scent for dogs or tracks in snow.
The hunters pour in from all directions
and carry home both bull and bear.

Why herdsmen who play on pipes are carried off

*It is fairly common knowledge that bears, like dolphins, deer, sheep,
calves, and even lambs, take great pleasure in musical tunes....*

Bears cannot help themselves when the multi-hued notes
of the shepherd's sackpipa swirl through the trees.
As if following the scent of honey,
bears track the tune.

Instead of leaping on the herdsman, the bear lifts him
and carries him into the woods while the piper must blow
without stopping to keep the bear's mood sweet.

When the bear grows hungry, as is its wont,
and drops his musician to search for food,
the herdsman exchanges pipes for horn and blows
such an ear-pounding din
that the bear dashes off in panic

and the man escapes back to his sheep
where he calls them close with a gentle tune
and moves to safer pasture until hunters kill the bear.

Household bears

*When they are still cubs they make wonderful, quite harmless play-
mates for the children of the household.*

The priest in the stone cathedral
warms his feet on the white skin
of a bear who fishes beneath ice,
offered by the devout shivering in the pews.

If a woman disappears, she has been taken by a bear.
If parts of a man lie shredded and bloody
on the path from one village to another,
he has been eaten by a bear.

Children and cubs tumble safely together
until they shed their unknowing
like a bear's winter fat and emerge
ravenous, into the uncertain spring.

III. GREATNESS IN THE LEAST INSTRUMENTS
Samuel Purchas

Salamander

*Man is unable to communicate successfully with the salamanders,
owing to the fiery element in which they dwell.* Attributed to
Paracelcus, 16th century

The myths still flicker in people's minds
that the salamander lives in fire
that his venom will poison the fruit
of any tree he climbs.
Some say the salamander's cold nature
will relieve a fever
but one drop of his venom
will leave a person hairless.

At night he makes himself visible
as a small ball of light running over fields
or peering into houses.
By day he never leaves his den
but in storms and great rain.

From the boil and clatter of human noise
he noses into humus above the delicate
sounds of earthworms
decomposing the dead.
If you put your hand on the forest floor and feel
a place colder than the rest,
a salamander is below.
At night his spots reflect moonlight
like stars planted in the cold
vast sky where voices go nowhere
and all fire dies.
But listen

On the Way Out

Vox es praeterea nihil. Samuel Purchas, *Purchas His Pilgrimage*, 1624

Someone usually calls a "Don't forget to"
but this time I'm leaving you

the sorting. Recycle my paper,
every old letter and manuscript

but keep the will and ten years'
tax returns. Keep the dogs' records.

You might want something of your dad;
he's compressed into three files. Let the yearbooks go.

I really don't care if you talk
to whatever of my brain function remains.

I'll want birdsong, the cheeps and twitters dying
down to a tethering thread to float me off

in the endless complexity
of each random note, each a full color spectrum

of the world in a millisecond, gone
before we know what we have heard.

Dumbfounded Goats

*If you catch hold of a goat's beard at the extremity…all the compan-
ion goats will stand stock still, staring at this particular goat in a
kind of dumbfounderment.* Aristotle

The field not to our taste,
we followed the ram around
broken fence boards and down a street
where wild rose and nasturtium tasted of perfume,
and peppery marigolds seasoned
the short but tender grass.

We spread out, nobody running,
among the people and dogs—we touched noses.
One person flapped us away;
others laughed and scratched our backs
but we could not stop roaming.

Searching for another fence
to show us where to be,
we circled and bunched,
wandered up and down
the hard road between green lawns,
tasted more bushes and plants, many new to us.

We floated out of our ordinary days
until the truck came
with the chute to guide us
and the man seized the ram by his beard
and all of us stilled, wondering
at where we were
and how we'd been led to confusion.

Invasive Species

These are terrible and fearefull to sight, and yet not hurtfull...
Gonzalo Fernández de Oviedo, *General and Natural History of
the Indies,* 1525

A cold Florida winter knocked green iguanas off their trees
to sidewalks, then commercial freezers
the reptile mind winding down
from its pineal eye's tracking light overhead
every cell slowing.

They never find out they are dying,
these creatures looking oddly human
splayed on their backs
four limbs extended
and soft bellies exposed to every cat or shoe.
Their deaths are impersonal, a cleaning up
of animals who never belonged
within these borders

former pets tossed
outdoors where they discovered
a wealth of greenery to eat—all our
flowers, shrubs, vegetables, and fruit
pickings from which they multiplied.

Burrowing under sidewalks, foundations,
seawalls, they speed up
the general collapse of our lives
when the usual bit of planet under our feet
gets tricky. We can't trust it

not to cave like soufflé
or heave us over the edge,
we reptiles losing our grip.

The Versatility of the Hedgehog

This animal is not, as many of us imagine, entirely useless to man.
Pliny the Elder

Wives and slaves,
examine carefully the hedgehogs
you find in the market
and do not let a merchant's smile seduce you to damaged
goods.
The skin that looks whole
may rot in your hands and lose its quills
if the hedgehog was caught after discharging
its corrosive urine upon itself,
enduring the pain of broken flesh
in a desperate attempt to make itself valueless.

Like the beaver, the animal knows why it is hunted.
After capture it must be hung
by one hind leg until it dies of hunger,
the body desiccated and clean, the quills strong for carding.

The hedgehog will cure many conditions
without the use of vain doctors
who strut and gather crowds on the street
as if they were actors or chariot drivers.
The flesh will treat and, some say, ward off
obstructions of the bladder; but beware:
if the animal has discharged its urine upon its body,
those who eat the flesh will suffer strangury.
Buy only from the merchants who guarantee their goods.

For its gall bladder to cure skin lesions and warts
or serve as a depilatory when mixed
with bats' brains and goats' milk,
the animal must be fresh-killed with one blow to the head.
The dried flesh taken with food will cure dropsy.
The ashes applied with oil prevent miscarriage and spasms.
Mixed with honey, they will restore hair to the body
where scarring has prevented its growth.

This humble animal lays up food for the winter
by rolling on fallen apples,
piercing one with his quills and taking another in his mouth
to his den. Whichever door he blocks up,
from that direction the next wind will come
heralding for you the change of season.

The Physic of Toads

Toad…the most noble kinde of Frog, most venomous and remarkable for courage and strength. Edward Topsell

To ward off contagion, carry a dried toad.

A dried toad steeped in vinegar and laid to the forehead
stops bleeding at the nose—
fear of a beast so contrary to human nature
constrains the blood to run into its proper place.

In the presence of poison at your table, a toad will change
        color.

If someone offend a toad, she gathers air into her body
and sighs out that poisoned breath
as near the offending person as she can get
and thus has her revenge.
If air causes blindness or dizziness, seek the toad.

A toad rubbed against a sprain will relieve the swelling.

How is it that in men's stomachs are found frogs and toads?
The evil happens to men who drink water
for from the water, toad eggs slip into the stomach
where they cleave fast and grow without air
as do all the evils of the psyche.

To cast out the toads, disembowel a serpent,
cut off the head and tail, cut the body into small pieces
and soak in water until the fat rises to the surface.
By drinking this and vomiting, the man will void all the toads
before they release their venom and kill him.

Toads dried and beaten to powder make strong poison of
      wine.

After eating toads, the bears of Pamphilia
being killed by men do poison their eaters.
If an asp eat a toad, its bite is incurable.
The stork will not eat a toad except in famine
at which it becomes as poisonous as the toad.
Any animal may harbor the toad's venom.

There is no ward against toads.

The Cinnamon Trade

Another account is also given, that a share is assigned to the sun…
and bursts out in flames of its own accord. Pliny the Elder

Herodotus

These curls of brown bark stirred in our wine
journey from conflict
in the farthest south where Dionysus grew up.

Birds greater than eagles collect the sticks
from hidden places and carry them high
on sheer rock cliffs to build their nests.

The Arabians gather dead oxen and other beasts of burden,
cut them into large hunks,
and place them at the foot of those cliffs. They hide

until the birds plunge straight down
with the force of falling boulders
and surge back up grasping animal parts the weight of men.

Their nests fail under the burden of this gift,
and shatter on the ground far below
with eggs, young, and cinnamon.

The birds leap high, and safely now the men
collect the spice and ship it where
our servants will adorn our food and wine.

Pliny

A glass or two of wine
will convince Herodotus of any whim
above prosaic fact. Cinnamon grows on a shrub,
three feet high at most in the far south-east,
and made difficult to get only by brambles among the plants.
Ethiopians sacrifice forty-four oxen, goats, and rams
to gain leave from Jove, whom they call Assabinus,
to harvest the twigs.
Priests set aside the god's portion
which bursts into flame in the sun
while—no surprise—middlemen take the rest,
shipping it to the port of the Gebbanites.

Here the traders dawdle, selling
cinnamon for glass and copper,
clothing, buckles, bracelets and necklaces,
all the things their women demand
if those men who survive the voyage
want a welcome on their return.

The price rose like Herodotus' birds
when the cinnamon forests were burnt
by enraged barbarians—rumor claims.
I cannot say if they protested some injustice
exercised by those in power
or if the southern winds of summer grew so hot
as to set fire to the earth, consuming
and making dear the spices
we will not do without.

Magpies

If you did not see me, you would deny that I am a bird. Martial,
Epigrams, 80 CE

A voice tells you to pull up your pants.
Stop frowning. Look alive!
No one's up there,
no microphone on a branch or floating angel.

The voice follows you down the street
where trees bubble into pink blossoms,
says the news is grim, the empire will fall.
A charlatan augur, it's a woman, a man.

When you hear your name
you think someone has set you up
and could be recording your stumbling pirouette,
your eyes erratic as bugs. You'll be a meme.

Or your ears shaped the rush and click
of passing cars into words, the mind knitting
a pattern of nonsense into sentences
the way one person's warning becomes conspiracy

plotting the source of all pain;
the mind craves order from the random indifference
of even the wet splat on your head
from the black and white birds above.

Only Ducks

Only ducks and birds of the same kind soar up straight away, ...and consequently they alone when they have fallen into the pits that we use for trapping wild animals get out again. Pliny the Elder

You stare skyward and know
chewing off your leg will not get you out of this trap.

Think of the good: this trap
is not lined with stakes.

You might think if you had a long stake
you could climb out or occupy yourself with trying

but if you spend all day trying
and failing, what will you make of your life?

If you die here, what has your life
meant in the world but that of any animal

earthbound in its animal
desires and destined to end in a pit?

You were not ready, no one was ready, for this pit
from which all you can see are ducks soaring skyward.

On the Sensibilities of Sheep

The sheep is said to be naturally dull and stupid. Of all quadrupeds it is the most foolish. Aristotle

The day the ram stepped through the spaces
in the cattle grid, we stepped after—
as the goats, cows and even the dog could not—
to the grass and new clover in the town square.

People bleated at us and dogs barked.
Strangers, we owed them nothing.
We chewed grass and our thoughts
of wandering. We prefer to stay
at the place where we arrive, if we are together.

The shepherd heaved us into his truck
as if we could not remember the way home.
We read his face, the mouth-corners skipping up,
and went to him willingly. We saw the cattle grid
pass easily beneath us. This time he shut the gate

and set the dog in motion,
tick tick at our legs,
the black eye promising calamity
and the blue warding it off.

The sun never sets faster or slower
but man and dog barked
to hurry us, neat and close,
into the corral for the night.

I woke and saw none of us,
even the field gone
as if I were falling down a rift
farther and farther from my herd,
tiny glints far above.

The loneliness carved out my heart
and I cried for my companions
until their bodies pressing soft against mine
gave me back to myself.

Herodotus Reports the Tale of the Phoenix

...for the people of Heliopolis are said to be the most learned of the Egyptians. Herodotus, *Histories*, 425 BCE

What creatures live in the deepest ocean
only the gods know. No man alive
admits meeting Poseidon.
The people of Heliopolis tell of a bird, sacred to them,
which arrives every five hundred years.
I have not seen the phoenix but in a painting
where it resembles an eagle feathered gold and red.

Many creatures arise without copulation
and birth. Surely everyone has seen
the worms that emerge from dung.
And consider the butterfly. In ordinary process
it begins in a cabbage leaf
as a worm smaller than a grain of millet.
There it grows into a grub, then a caterpillar.
Late in the season, the caterpillar builds a chrysalis
from which bursts the winged insect.

Thus the phoenix emerges from his dead father
and shapes an egg out of myrrh—
if common birds build intricate nests,
surely a phoenix might shape an egg with his beak.
He grasps the egg with his long toes
and, proving he can fly a distance with its weight,
returns to the nest and hollows it out
to place his father's corpse inside. Sealed,
the weight now equals that of the solid egg.
He carries the egg from Arabia high over the mountains
to the Temple of the Sun where, the priests say,
he places it on the altar as an offering to the gods

bringing good fortune to Heliopolis.
I have seen evidence of fantastic beings—
a water-dwelling lizard called the crocodile,
the bones of winged serpents;
but I must acknowledge the phoenix
like the Oracle at Delphi in her many guises
or the gods hidden on Olympus
may forever tantalize my imaginings.

Oviedo Encounters the Sloth in Brazil

*The first invention of Musicke might seeme by the hearing of this
beast, to have the first principles of that Science, rather then by any
other thing in the World.* Gonzalo De Oviedo

Its four limbs cannot carry it on earth
but drag the body with birdlike claws,
belly weaving a trail in the dust.

Too slow for sport, with a mouth too small to bite,
it does not defend itself from capture
or bring any profit yet known to man.

It cannot be hurried, can never be hurried

by threats or sticks even when it sees a tree
where its one desire is to climb
with long arms and claws that reach slowly
as if through honey to the highest branch

where it is lost in quietude
among leaves and birds. No one has seen it eat
anything but air, as it turns its face to the wind,
a round child's face with a dark stroke across each eye

painted carelessly, an animal half-formed, a friend of darkness,

quiet by day but singing at night
six notes up the scale and down
as a man may sing do, re, me, fa, so, la
this creature calls ah, ah, ah, ah, ah, ah in perfect pitch

composing the music of this New World
and all the marvels in it.

Quadruped Sleep

*It would appear that not only do men dream, but horses also, and
dogs, and oxen; aye, and sheep, and goats, and all viviparous quad-
rupeds; and dogs show their dreaming by barking in their sleep.*
Aristotle

Horse
A hat walks under my chin
I lift with the ends of my teeth
and a boy's face tips up
the mouth round and so close
that I could eat his breath

I see a dark thing twisting at the edge of vision
my back legs dance sideways when the front pull straight

In distance even stone walls shrink like a day going past
it comes back in pieces
the hayrack's full

Ox
the shoulders ache and the neck

we pull the earth to order
ruts in the field heave under our hooves

when my partner stumbles my head bows with his

a soft breeze, a place without flies
now I bow my head freely to the grass

Goat
Somebody's kicking, skin twitches
my legs want to jump
blackberry vines perfume the mouth

I climb past a fence, up a mountain and see
down the other side the same bracken I've left

I leap into wilderness
my ears catch the air like wings

Sheep
I listen for our safety
the others' breath a low song
night rolls out its dampness
a bowl of stars cups our heads

Dog
clotting stink of raccoon in the plum tree
I leap that high

chickens squawk and flap across the yard
my teeth snap on a feather's edge

when the phantom pack races
the night sky, I howl with it

until human voices call
my wild song into their lighted room

IV. THAT SCIENCE IS DIVINE
Edward Topsell

Paradise

The explorers are devoured by such a passion to discover this strait that
they risk a thousand dangers; for it is certain that he who does discover
it—if it ever is discovered—will obtain the imperial favour, not to men-
tion great authority. Peter Martyr, letter written 1504

I. Antonio Pigafetta to the most illustrious and excellent Lord,
Philippe Villiers de l'Isle-Adam, renowned grand master of
Rhodes:

September, 1519

We held it most certain that the islands called the Moluccas
in which all spices are produced, lay within the Spanish western
and not the Portuguese eastern half of the globe.
Not knowing whether ingenious Nature
had opened a passage through the southern continent,
Ferdinand Magellan determined to follow the sun west
to the source of spices and west again home
where, rebuffed by his king, he had sworn loyalty to Spain
as I to his command;
but the Spanish captains of the other four ships
whispered malice against their Portuguese captain-general.

We stopped to load our ships at the Canaries
where, your Lordship must know, one island has no water
until each midday a cloud descends around a large tree,
saturating the leaves to such extent
that enough water to supply all the men and animals
falls below like Pliny's perpetual fountain.

Sailing down the coast of Ghinea, concealed from the Portuguese,
we saw large fish with terrible teeth
who devour men alive or dead. We caught them with iron hooks

but even the small ones were not good to eat.
Of the many birds, one kind had no anus and another no feet
who always lives on the sea, and fish leaped and flew
packed so many together as to resemble an island.

II. Rio de Janeiro Bay, Dec. 1519

The people have an infinite number of parrots
and gave us eight or ten for one mirror
and little monkeys with delicate hands
that look like lions, golden-haired,
with manes standing high around their faces
like the collars of dignitaries.
The men traded us one or two of their daughters
as slaves for one hatchet, but they would not give us their wives.
For a playing card, they gave me five fowls
and even thought they cheated me.
These people could be converted easily to the faith.

Our captain-general explored Rio de la Plata
where Juan Diaz de Solis had been eaten by cannibals.
We would have captured one
but they fled with great leaps into the trees.

III. Bahia de los Patos [Duck Bay] Feb. 1520

Nearing the pole, we anchored at two islands
full of sea-wolves and fat black geese in such abundance
that we filled the five ships in an hour.
The geese do not fly but swim and eat fish.
The sea-wolves have faces like calves
with small, round ears and large teeth. They have no legs
but only feet attached to the body. They would be fierce
if they could run. We suffered a great storm
until St. Elmo, St. Nicholas, and St. Clara appeared

on the yardarms, upon which the storm ceased.
Many seamen would attest to the miracle
had they lived.

IV. Wintering at Port St. Julian, Patagonia, March—August

Our clever captain-general tricked two giants
into capture by filling their hands with gifts
and quickly clapping irons around their legs. One pleaded so
by signs to bring his wife that a party went to fetch her,
but fighting broke out. One sailor died immediately
an arrow struck his leg. Our cross-bows and guns
hit no one, for they leaped about and ran faster than horses.
We buried our comrade
and burned the house where they stored their goods.

The two giants ate a basketful of biscuit
and rats without skinning them.
These people clip their hair like monks' tonsures.
When one dies, they say a dozen painted devils appear
and dance around the dead man
throwing fire from their mouths and rumps.

They were meant as a prize for our king
but did not live long aboard ship. The one
with whom I exchanged words—*capae* for bread
and *oli* for water uttered deep in the throat—
became a Christian before his death and thus was saved.
The captain-general named those people *Patagones*.

We sheltered in the bay all winter. Looking
to future needs, Captain-General cut rations of wine and biscuit
to the anger of many, especially the Spanish,
who lacked his faith in a southern passage.

They roused their unlettered shipmen to mutiny
but our captain-general defeated them
and quartered the dead bodies of two, as was custom,
spearing them up for a lesson.

Finally, in August, four ships weighed anchor,
one having broken up but all men saved by a miracle.
We banished two unrepentant mutineers and shuddered to hear
their cries and prayers as we sailed out
to the terrible storms of that sea.

V. The Strait of Magellan, 1520

On the Festival of the Eleven Thousand Virgins
we entered a strait and followed a maze
of inlets and outcroppings overhung by clouds
and giant birds watching us for carrion.
Blue walls of ice moaned as if ready to fall.
At a thick forest we ate a sweet herb
as there was nothing else but fish.
But never did we turn wrong or lose the way
thanks to the captain-general's skill.
And when we reached the western sea
all wept for joy and the blessing on our mission.

We had thought to reach the Islands in weeks
but in four months saw no land
in the calm emptiness we named *Pacific*.
We ate biscuit reduced to crumbs, grub-filled
and stinking of rats' dirt. Our water turned to slime.
We soaked ox hides in sea water,
then warmed and ate them, though some men
had teeth so loosened in swollen gums they could not chew.
We ate the rats. Many men sickened; some died
and if our Lord and his Mother had not aided us

by guiding us to an island where we found provisions,
we should all have died in this vast sea.
I think that never again will man undertake this voyage.

We stopped at the islands of Mazzaua and Gatighan
where we saw pigeons, doves, turtledoves, parrots, and bats
the size of eagles. We had time to kill but one
which tasted of chicken. All the people chew betel;
it reddens the mouth and teeth but cools the heart.
Without it, they would die.

VI. The Philippines, befriending the Rajah of Cebu and fighting on Mactan, April, 1521

They killed our mirror, our light, our comfort, and our true guide.
Antonio Pigafetta

Eighteen months after setting out, we landed for a month at Cebu
where our captain befriended the King Humabon,
converting him to the true faith
along with all his people, who had worshipped only the sky—
to the delight of the shipmen,
for the captain had forbidden intimacy with heathen.
This king declared undying friendship to ours, as a son to a father.

At this island are large sea-snails that kill whales
when swallowed. They leave their shells
and eat the whale's heart. They have black teeth and skin
inside a white shell and are good to eat.
Every night at midnight when we were in that city,
a black bird like a crow
flew over the houses and began to screech,
setting the dogs howling. The uproar lasted four hours
but the people would not tell us a reason.

So successful was he in acquiring Christians and gold
from among the heathen
that the captain-general believed himself
a weapon of God. I say this to none but myself:
I feared his passion to save immortal souls
drove him to neglect our mission for the glory and profit of Spain.
He vowed to convert King Humabon's enemies
by friendship or sword, but the people of neighboring Mactan
would not bow to anyone.

Wrapped in his faith,
our captain led us to war
where, overwhelmed by their numbers,
he was cut to pieces and some few of us escaped.
We offered the heathens ransom to return him for Christian burial
but no amount would pry away their trophy.

He had endured hunger without weakening,
led us safe through storms, and navigated the unknown
more truly than any man in the world.
Such a soul finds its way quickly to heaven
though the body lies scattered in unconsecrated ground.

VII. Moluccan Islands, November, 1521

After wandering from island to island like Odysseus,
seeing gold and elephants, figs half a cubit long,
and leaves that walk, we reached Tidore
and all the wealth of spices.
I went ashore to see how cloves grow
nowhere else in the world but these five
mountains on five islands,
tipping the wide-spread branches.
They sprout white, ripen to red, and dry to black.
Every day a cloud descends and encircles

first one and then another mountain,
whereby the cloves become perfect.

Declaring himself a servant of the King of Spain,
the Sultan of Bacchian filled our ships with cloves.
He also gave us beautiful dead birds
of a kind never before seen. The size of thrushes
with small heads and long beaks like crows,

they have no feet or wings
but thick plumes on their sides,
glowing gold when turned in the sunlight.
The bodies are a velvet brown with cream-colored heads
and deep green throats akin to emeralds.

The birds never rest on the ground nor anything that grows
but spend their lives floating in the sky like clouds,
their gauzy plumes spread behind them
hidden from the sight of everyone but God
until they fall dead into human hands,
bringing signs of Paradise to earth.

VIII. *Vittoria* **alone reaches Seville in 1522 with eighteen
men of an original 250.**

We carried home five of these birds,
and did not stop
at the island of cinnamon, the other of sandalwood,
an island of people no taller than a cubit
and with ears as long as themselves.
We passed an island all of women
who become pregnant by the wind
and another with birds that carry buffaloes.
Our remaining ship eluded the Portuguese threat
of capture along their African coast

as if the birds, as they were said to do,
kept us safe in war.

With nothing but rice and water,
some wanted to put ashore
where we would be imprisoned, but we
who loved honor more than life
kept on, though twenty-one men died.
When we cast the dead into the sea,
the Indians sank face downward to embrace the deep
but the Europeans sank with faces up
as if longing, not for cloves or wealth,
but for the birds who would bring us Paradise.

A Llama Decides to Sit

The Pacos will grow reastie under their burthens, lying down, and will endure to be cut in a thousand pieces before they will rise when this humor takes them. Joseph de Acosta, *Natural and Moral History of the Indies*, 1590

And the whole caravan halts,
the jingles and creaks, the sighs and voices.
Behind us the city where men work like mules
carrying silver out of the mountain, where
streams from the mint run silver with mercury
and ahead the city of our destination
where we will load the bars onto Spanish ships
are weeks away.

He folds himself down
with head raised on its long neck
to watch clouds heave and spread
across snowy mountains cut against the horizon
falling to brown hills heaped like dried mud
and down to the valley of scrub embroidered on rubble.

We know nothing will shift the llama,
neither whips nor curses, as nothing
shifts the god in the mountain that swallows men.

The llama's eyes and nostrils open on a clean wind.
An ear twitches toward my voice
as I praise his brow, his lashes
in rhythm with the sun's whisper
over his body, in rhythm with the clouds
opening and closing
until the wind dies to a tickle
and the distance around us

enters us, our lives
becalmed on the edge
of a mountain path just wide enough for a llama.

Jean De Léry Confronts a Monster

Not only are [the Tupinamba] utterly ignorant of the sole and true
God; what is more…they neither confess nor worship any gods,
either of heaven or of earth.

Rashly we set forth without a guide
and lost our way in a valley
where the trees stood back
and the underbrush whispered.

When we heard rustling on a rise, we hoped
a savage out hunting would reveal himself
and guide us back to the village.
Instead, thirty feet away, a fearsome lizard
bigger than a man, with scales as sharp as oyster shells
and burning eyes, rose from the greenery.

Days before, when thunder set the savages trembling,
we declared it a sign of the true god whose grandeur
shook heaven and earth. They said
a god who frightens is good for nothing.
We have work ahead to bring them to Truth

but may make inroads through their belief in souls.
The virtuous who avenge themselves and eat their enemies
retire to an Elysian field behind the high mountains
while the worthless ones who turn the other cheek
are trapped by the devil in eternal agony.

Now we three had not even a pistol, only swords, puny
against the furious and well-armed animal.
It opened its maw to pant like a dragon.
We froze,
lest a twitch arouse it to run us down and devour us.

A full quarter-hour it stared
until turning, immense tail crashing
through leaves and branches, it swarmed uphill
while we slumped to our knees with thanks for deliverance.

Later I recalled that lizards delight
in looking at a human face.
If so, this one took its fill of pleasure
in gazing at us while we nearly emptied our bowels
before this prospect of hell.

Father Acosta Ponders the Divinity of Dung

I have considered this, wondering at the providence of the Creator,
who hath so appointed, that all Creatures should serve Man.

Birds of these forests range
in colors that
no painter can capture—
tawny orange turning gold, the green of new grass.
The Indians make portraits out of feathers
taken from parrots, *Tomineios* the size of bees
and all between

fitted with such precision and illusion
of life
that only touch will confirm
the medium. Looked at directly,
the portraits glow with a luster lit by holiness,
yet angled differently, they turn
dark and dull as if
to remind us of mortality.

Of the same country are ill-favored
birds, black and white
with long beaks and bodies shaped like gourds
living on islands appearing like snow-capped mountains
drifted seawards from the Andes
but they are all dusty dung
the Indians call *guano.* Men row to the islands
to take shares allotted by the Emperor and fertilize the valleys
where quinces, pomegranates, and other fruits grow
in such bounty as appeared in Eden.

When the islands blacken with nesting birds
the people are forbidden on pain of death
from disturbing them,
so valued are these birds
and their excrement
more than all the gold
we have taken from this New World.

Iguana Raid, Chichirivchi

*With slave raiders and merchants (both legal and illegal) regularly
assaulting the region, the friars were unable to create and maintain
stable relationships with Tierra Firme's indigenous inhabitants.*
Erin Stone, *Slave Raiders vs. Friars: Tierra Firme, 1513—1522*

Lying in our stone cells at night, we hear
their claws whisper against packed dirt,
like an encroaching army creeping from the trees

to invade the fields we've cleared and planted,
our labor, faith made visible
in the cucumbers and sweet melons

the iguanas will ravage.
We must get up once more
as if called too early to morning prayer

a dancing, shouting prayer with sticks and brooms
to sweep away the hellish creatures,
their backs ridged with spikes, their sharp teeth.

They have come from the sea grottos where they grow
on whatever the tide brings to this hissing horde
that scurries into the trees after desecrating our crops.

Laughing at our fear, the Indians pick them up by the neck
and the reptiles open their mouths as if to bite
but go limp like geese.

Indeed they are like geese to these natives
who roast and eat them, as others do their enemies,
sharing with us the white, mild flesh

until the communion breaks, the animals
claim our fields, and the Indians must hide
in the trees like iguanas about to be taken.

Yellow Bird

*You would think that he was dressed in golden cloth below, and clad
in a mantle of violet damask above; one is enraptured by his beauty.*
Jean de Léry

Anyone can enter
where friars built a gold
church against the sky—
apostate and believer,
Indian and European.
Saints and cherubs
grow on the walls, their gilded faces
reflecting pale light.
Year by year, the forest
recedes from the church compound
and the slave pillory in the square.
The desert grows.

In the forest,
the bird carries sun and sky down
to the canopy where we look
up at its light, the yellow-gold breast,
the long blue tail. Its black beak,
big as a fist, shines like polish.
The Tupi sing *canidé-iouve heuraouech*
calling the birds to flock in the village trees

and down to their houses
when bats and owls spread night
through the forest where
the jaguar tracks a peccary herd
to their burrows. The chorus
of clicking tusks warns him
back to his tree,

its silver moonlight,
where he waits.

Just before yellow birds raise the day,
the first peccaries till the forest floor,
their scrub-brush coats
the colors of shadow and dirt.
The jaguar takes his,
the people theirs.

Sunlight gilds the canopy,
threads through leaves and branches,
touches us and fades
like Tupi songs. Time,
always hungry,
enters.

"A Four-Footed Strange Beast"
Edward Topsell

We shared some alarm
at the Almighty's piecing together a creature
from the scraps of others.
It is the size of a cat with a mallard's bill,
feet cloven into parts like a dog's,
a long neck, and the tail of a lizard. It is shelled
like a lobster or barded horse
with only the pointed ears unguarded.

Some affirm it has a voice like a swine
but not the meat, though Don Oviedo declares
the meat superior to that of kids—
if one wants to eat goat like the Spanish
who, in their superstition, thought the beast
sent to earth to test us.
Or so I am told.

Being of many parts, the beast has many names:
Tatus, Guinean Beast, Aiochtochth, Armato, Bardati;
but I believe it to be a Brasilian hedgehog
for the way it draws up within its armor
as a hedgehog does in its prickled skin
and thus is no great mystery.

Obtaining one from unknown source,
Marcellus the Apothecary of Ulmes stuffed it
for exhibition. Ladies,
after their initial faintness,
took to wearing hats and cloaks
pieced of stiff cloth like scales.

Only last year merchants brought the living creatures
to London's wealthy estates where they wandered
among the gillyflowers and destroyed garden worms
until the winter damp killed them
and some settled into jars
on basement shelves of the science museum.

Ornithologist George Edward Describes
the Ash-Colored Parrot

I doubt not but this trade seems very barbarous to you, but since
it is followed by mere necessity, it must go on.... Captain Willem
Bosman, transporter of slaves, 1705

The bigness of a tame Pigeon, the Bird
is ash-colored with a short red tail
and the under-feathers when examined
leave a finest powder on the fingers.
The legs and feet are formed as in other Parrots
but the scaly skin is black.

I drew this Bird from life, and it survives
as property of Sir Hans Sloane.
Although this Bird does not sing
and has a voice of natural harshness,
it greets its Master and repeats his words.

These Parrots are known in London as Guinea Birds,
coming from the Coast of Africa
and brought here by the Traders
that supply our Sugar Islands with Negroes
and increase their incomes
by gathering additional Exotics on their way.

Birds in the Moon

...their chearefulness seems to intimate, that they have some noble design in hand...namely, to get above the admosphere, hie and fly away to the other world. Charles Morton, 1684

During a full moon in autumn
I watched geese in their V formation flying upwards
into the pale light, their leisurely wingbeats
disguising great speed.

We have traced the life histories of beasts, insects, and fish.
We discovered industrious cities in a drop of water
and mapped the circulation of blood in our bodies,
but the destination of birds in winter eluded us.

Now we turn our eyes to the Heavens and see
the moon is to earth as earth is to the moon
in the planets' sojourn through the heavens, for the Creator
would not fashion a world without someone to live on it.

Where else should birds' upward flight take them
but to the moon? They swing on fast asleep,
living off their own fat for the two-month journey
without gravity to slow them.

Through the telescope we see dark patterns of water
and lighter shapes of hills
all pale and silvery, the water somber gray
and the trees shifting from gilt to slate.

Here, migrating birds acquire new feathers
and blend with the trees
drowsily eating fruit and insects
before the long flight back to earth

and all the work of begetting and raising young.
I seek funds to train twenty-five cranes
to carry me to the moon in a basket,
to fashion wings from swans' feathers
to speed me past earth's gravity,
to explore the moon's terrain and search out its inhabitants—
gifts of beads, which have proved useful to earthly travelers,
        should suffice—
to chart the course so that others may come after me
and enrich our country through trade.
When the cranes notice a change in air and abatement of food,
they will carry me home
where I will write a full account for the Royal Society
and the edification of the public.

I remind you that the Age of Exploration is in its infancy
and we may solve one of Creation's great mysteries,
as did Copernicus, Kepler and Galileo,
if we discard our insular belief in Earth's supremacy
and follow the natural inclination of birds
into the Moon's embrace.

A History of the Pigeon

"Everybody is interested in pigeons." Rev. Whitwell Elwin, 1859

1.
The congregation rises for a dove and a chorus.
Pigeons dribble archaeological strata
on the shoulders of statues. A pigeon is
a dove. The dodo was a pigeon.

She stood beside his corpse on the roadside, feathers rising
in the wind of passing cars,
her long stare, days until the attachment ebbed
and she flew or died.

2.
If you be infected with the plague,
wrap with warm bricks
and apply to the sores a live pigeon
cut in two parts.

Doves kiss continually but are chaste.
Taught to beguile wild pigeons
in the likeness of friendship, they lead them
into the fowler's net and destruction.

The meat is most tender at four weeks.
The best sauce for pigeons is vinegar and butter melted
and parsley roasted in their bellies.
Cover in a clay pot and do not overcook.

3.
Loving the place where they were first fed,
pigeons will fly home even from a far country,
but they carry no letter without peril
for that letter is oft the cause and occasion of their death.

Released, they spiral and circle a sky
etched with magnetic lines and carrying waves of sound
from deep in oceans and earth. When signals rebound
from familiar terrain, they fly true to home.

4.
Pigeons can learn to distinguish
Monet from Picasso, Impressionist from Cubist.
Upside-down Picasso is still Picasso
but Monet's water cannot be sky.

The city pigeon tailored in grey like a lawyer
with a silk tie shifting colors as she walks
finds minute evidence in a sidewalk.
She absorbs memories carried in passing cars.

5.
I watch the city scrolling away behind me,
a dead mate,
a patient red eye.

Jean Baptiste van Helmont Explains Abiogenesis, 17th Century

Animals and plants come into being in earth and in liquid because there is water in earth, and air in water, and in all air is vital heat so that in a sense all things are full of soul. Aristotle

In Egypt after Nile floods, the people thought mice
grew from silt, nose first toward air
where they dried and breathed in life
before fattening themselves in the fields of corn and wheat.
We may have doubted, but I have succeeded in their generation,
not with Nile silt but this clay pot.

My previous experiment growing and measuring a tree in a
      large pot
for five years showed plants feed on water and light, unlike
      mice
and other animals that sexually reproduce or generate
spontaneously from what only appears to be empty air.
Now I have shown how a sweaty shirt, open pot, and wheat
combined their forces to activate life.

It is well known that worms hatch from mud, and fireflies gain
      life
in morning dew. Consider, then, how this clay pot
acts as the enclosure for the fumes from wheat
grains and a worn shirt to become the leavening force
      producing mice
with the help of whatever is found in my shed's air.
The pressure of one animating force against another generates

the creature that may afterwards reproduce for generations
in the usual way. Such is the versatility of life
and the mystery of all we cannot see in air

and earth as represented by this humble pot
from which emerged, in twenty-one days, three mice
suggesting, as you may surmise, the shape and color of wheat.

Truly we may say that wheat
sustains all. Unknown still are degree and moisture needed to
      generate
such lower forms of mammals as mice
and what might be the chemicals in human sweat that kindle
      life
in the warming stillness of the open pot.
We must ask what other properties or molecules does air

conduct? Perhaps molecules from everything on earth drift in
      air
and gather to their destined form. Wheat
and cotton grow with sun and water; we forge our pots
from earth and fire. The four elements provide the spark to
      generate
the process of combustion that builds to life
perpetual in seeds, eggs, parents, and autogenesis, as with our
      mice.

Nothing then is lost; the vital heat survives in air, wheat,
cloth, mice, the very clay on which we stand or dig for pots.
Beings generate in every combination, and everything on earth
      is life.

NOTES

The title is taken from Samuel Purchas, *Purchas His Pilgrimage,*
Book VIII,1625. Writing about hummingbirds in the New World,
he says:

> One would say, *Voxes, praetereanihil:* but so
> could not any truly say, for even otherwise is it
> almost miraculous: Nature making this little
> shop her great store-house of wonder, and
> astonishment, and shewing her greatest
> greatness in the least instruments.

Section I
Invocation from Ovid's Metamorphosis, Rolfe Humphries'
translation, 1955:

> My intention is to tell of bodies changed
> To different forms; the gods, who made the changes,
> Will help me — or so I hope — with a poem
> That runs from the world's beginning to our own days.

Goat in the Wilderness:

> Aaron shall bring forward the goat designated by lot
> for the Lord, which he is to offer as a sin offering; while
> the goat designated by lot for Azazel shall be left
> standing alive before the Lord, to make expiation
> with it and to send it off to the wilderness for Azazel.
> -*Leviticus 16:9-10* read on Yom Kippur

Section II
Lupus Est In Fabula is a proverb to be said when there is a sud-
den silence during conversation, translating as "the wolf is in
the tale"

Section III

On the Way Out: *Vox es praeterea nihil* translates as "You are nothing but a voice." Samuel Purchas quoting Plutarch when describing hummingbirds.

Dumbfounded Goats: *"About 100 goats are on the loose right now in a Boise neighborhood."* Joe Parris, KTVB

Only Ducks:
> Only ducks and birds of the same kind soar up straight away, and move skyward from the start, and this even from water; and consequently they alone when they have fallen into the pits that we use for trapping wild animals get out again. Pliny the Elder

Section IV

Paradise end note: Ferdinand Magellan, an expatriate Portuguese whose king had refused to fund such a venture, and the young King Charles I of Spain who became Charles V, Holy Roman Emperor, believed a westward passage would establish a Spanish claim to the Moluccas of Indonesia, although the Portuguese would claim them from the east.

Returning under the command of Basque navigator Juan Sebastian de Elcano, Vittoria (Victoria), the second smallest of the five ships, returned alone down the coast of Africa and around the Cape of Good Hope. The cloves on this one ship earned the expedition a profit. The *San Antonio* had deserted and sailed back to Spain. The *Santiago* was shipwrecked near Port St. Julian. After Magellan's death, the crews burned the *Concepciòn* because there were too few men to sail it. The flagship *Trinidad* with 60 men stayed behind in Indonesia for repairs. Only four of its men are known to have eventually returned to Spain. Father Acosta Ponders the Divinity of Dung: *Tomineios* are a type of hummingbird.

A History of the Pigeon: the Rev. Whitwell Elwin, an early reader of *On the Origin of Species,* recommending to publisher John Murray that Charles Darwin write about pigeons instead of *On the Origin of Species,* which would attract little notice.

ACKNOWLEDGMENTS

Arkana: Oviedo Encounters the Sloth in Brazil

Connecticut River Review: A Llama Decides to Sit

Gyroscope Review: On the Sensibilities of Sheep

Lights by Pleasure Boat Studio: Castor; Elephants, their Capacity; Scitalis; The Reverend Alexander Ross Explains Griffins; Saint Ambrose Admonishes

On the Seawall: The Monster Hyena, The Versatility of the Hedgehog, A Four-Footed Strange Beast, Lupus Est In Fabula

Pen and Brush: Pompey Takes Elephants to Rome for his Triumph Ceremony

The Lake: A Brief Account of Venomous Creatures, Of a Frog Lately Found in Ireland

The Ravensperch: Aristotle on the Disappearance of Birds, Ornithologist George Edwards Describes the Ash-Colored Parrot, The Cinnamon Trade

Sky Island Journal: Invasive Species

Swimm: A Bed Among Goats

Terrain: Quadruped Sleep

LIST OF WORKS CONSULTED

Dates are approximate, as they vary widely according to different sources. The first time a source appears in the book, the full source and date are given; after that only the author's name appears.

Herodotus, *Histories*, 425 BCE

Aristophanes, *Lysistrata*, 411 BCE

Aristotle, *History of Animals*, 350 BCE

Cicero, Letter to Marcus Marius at Cumae, 55 BCE

Strabo, *Geography*, 1st century CE

Pliny the Elder, *Natural History*, 77 CE

Martial, *Epigrams*, 80 CE

Gaius Julius Solinus, *The Wonders of the World*, 3rd century CE

Saint Ambrose of Milan, *Hexameron*, late 4th century CE

Saint Isidore, Archbishop of Seville, *Etymologies*, 7th century CE

Giraldus Cambrensis (Gerald of Wales) Topography of Ireland, 1188, and The Itinerary of Archbishop Baldwin through Wales, 1191

The Aberdeen Bestiary, 1200 CE

Paracelcus, a Swiss physician and alchemist, late 15th century

Antonio Pigafetta, *First Voyage Around the World*, 1525 (Journal of Magellan's Voyage)

Gonzalo Fernández de Oviedo y Valdés, *Natural History of the West Indies*, 1525

Peter Martyr (Pietro Martire d'Anghiera), *De Orbe Novo*, first published 1530
Gathered writings of many others, such as Acosta and Oviedo

Olaus Magnus, *A Description of the Northern Peoples*, 1555

Jean De Léry, *History of a Voyage to the Land of Brazil*, 1578

Joseph de Acosta, *Natural and Moral History of the Indies*, 1590

Edward Topsell, *The History of Four-Footed Beasts*, 1607

Samuel Purchas, *Purchas His Pilgrimage*, 1624

Alexander Ross, *Arcana Microcosmi*, 1652

Wolfgang Franz, *The History of Brutes*, pub. 1670

Captain Willem Bosman, *A new and accurate description of the coast of Guinea, divided into the Gold, the Slave, and the Ivory coasts*, 1705

Charles Morton, *An Enquiry into the Physical and Literal Sense of that Scripture*, 1684 or 1694

Erin Stone, *Slave Raiders vs. Friars: Tierra Firme, 1513—1522*, 2017

SHERRY RIND'S poetry books are *The Hawk in the Back Yard* (Anhinga Award), *A Fall Out the Door* (King County Arts Award, Confluence Press), and *Between States of Matter* (The Poetry Box Select, 2020). Chapbooks are The *Whooping Crane Dance* and *A Natural History of Grief.* She has received grants and awards from the Seattle and King County Arts Commissions, Pacific Northwest Writers, National Endowment for the Arts, and Artist Trust. Near Seattle, she lives with Airedale terriers, chickens, cockatiels, and a corn snake. She would like to keep a goat.

sherryrind.wixsite.com/writer